First published 1980 by Octopus Books Limited
59 Grosvenor Street, London W1

ISBN 0 7064 1383 0

Produced by Mandarin Publishers Limited
22a Westlands Road, Quarry Bay, Hong Kong

Printed in Hong Kong

PDO 80-303

By Royal Appointment

Jeffrey Archer

Illustrated by Peter Longden

OCTOPUS

'Which is the fastest car in Littleland?' asked Queen Echo, spreading some 'By Royal Appointment' marmalade on a burnt piece of toast. 'Which is the fastest car in Littleland?'

'I have absolutely no idea,' replied Good King Benefactor, not looking up from his morning copy of *The Crown News.*

'As King of Littleland you're supposed to know everything,' said Queen Echo. 'As King of Littleland you're supposed to know everything.'

'Am I really?' asked the King gloomily. He always disliked being asked difficult questions before he had finished his breakfast.

'Of course,' said the Queen. 'What would your subjects think if they asked you a simple question, and you didn't know the answer. What would your subjects think if they asked you a simple question, and you didn't know the answer.'

'But they never ask me anything,' replied the King.

'That's not the point,' said the Queen. 'So you had better find out the answer pretty quickly. It's just the sort of question someone might ask you.'

'How can I find out the answer,' replied the King quickly before the Queen could repeat herself, 'when no one ever tells me anything.'

'I'll ask the Lord Chancellor for you. He seems to know everything, and you can hide behind the throne and listen to what he has to say.'

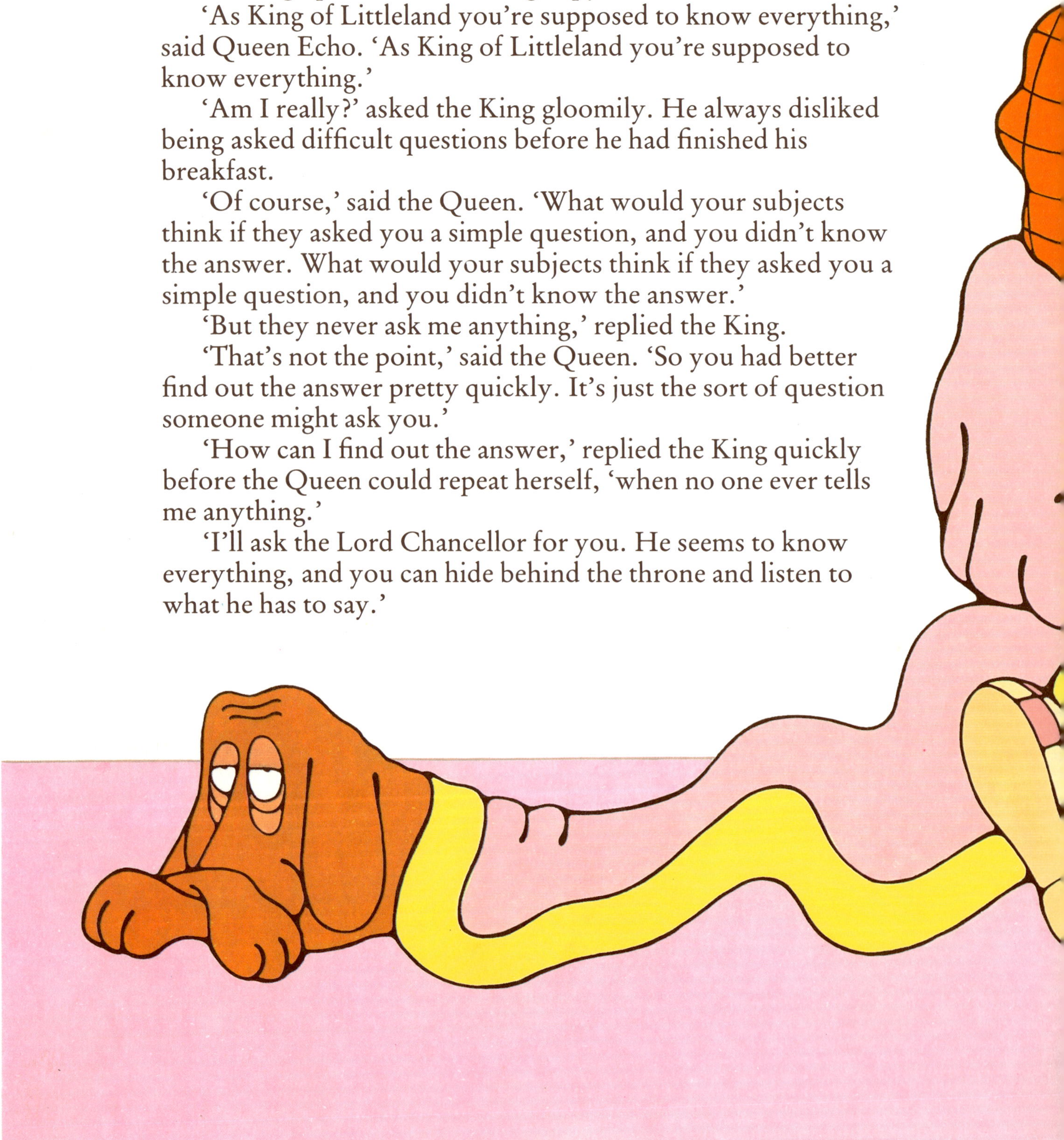

So the Queen went off to look for the Lord Chancellor (repeating herself as she went) because he was the only man who knew all the laws of Littleland off by heart, and many other useful facts as well. Meanwhile the King tried to hide behind the throne. But however small he attempted to make himself, his crown or his ermine-trimmed royal train always showed. A few blinks later, the Right Honourable Lord Chancellor of Littleland entered the throne room as quickly as he could, which was actually very slowly, because he was 210 years old.

'You sent for me, Your Majesty?' he said, bowing very low to the Queen.

'I did, I did,' she replied.

'She did, she did,' came a voice from behind the throne. The Queen and the Lord Chancellor pretended not to hear him.

'I wish to know, Lord Chancellor,' continued the Queen, 'which is the fastest car in Littleland? I wish to know, Lord Chancellor, which is the fastest car in Littleland?'

The old man leaned heavily on his stick (no one is allowed to sit while the Queen is standing), stroked his long white beard and considered the question very carefully. After a long pause, he surprised the Queen with his reply.

'Nobody can really be certain,' he declared.

'Then why should I be expected to know, if nobody else does,' demanded the King crawling out from his hiding place. '*Why* isn't anybody certain?'

'Why isn't anybody certain, why isn't anybody certain?' repeated Queen Echo.

'Nobody is certain, Your Majesties, because there has never been a race between all the cars in the kingdom.'

'Then it's high time there was one,' said the King.

'I am sure you are right, Your Majesty, and if that is your desire, I will issue a royal proclamation inviting all the cars in the country to compete in a Round Littleland Race.'

'What a good idea.'

'What a good idea. What a good idea.'

'And may I suggest to Your Majesty,' continued the Lord Chancellor, 'that you might award some special prize to the winner to mark the occasion – a gold cup perhaps.'

'Splendid. We shall do just that,' said King Benefactor, feeling very beneficent. 'It must be the biggest cup ever made in Littleland,' he added.

'Splendid. We shall do just that,' said the Queen. 'It will be the. . .'

'Yes, yes, my dear,' interrupted the King. The Queen fell silent for the first time in months.

'With your permission,' said the Lord Chancellor. 'I shall immediately instruct the Royal prizemaker to start work on the biggest cup ever seen in Littleland, as it will take some time to make.'

The King nodded quickly; it was the only way to keep the Queen silent.

The Queen nodded twice.

The Lord Chancellor left slowly.

Good King Benefactor spent the rest of the day writing out the formal invitations to all the cars in the kingdom to join him at the Palace for the big race. The King and Queen didn't actually live in a Palace, they lived in a salt-and-pepper-pot which all the citizens thought was a Palace (only the Lord Chancellor knew the truth). When the King had finished all the invitations they were sealed with the Royal stamp and delivered by the King's own special footmen, who were known as the Royal Males. Queen Echo spent her day planning out the route which all the cars should follow. She actually wanted the cars to go round Littleland twice, to be twice as sure of the winner, but the King was able to convince her that once round would be quite enough.

A few months later, when the biggest cup ever was ready, and every citizen of Littleland had turned out to watch, and red and white flags had been hung along the route, all the cars invited to participate in the race lined up outside the Salt-and-pepper-pot Palace for a Royal inspection.

There were seven cars in all:
the Speedy Car
the Flashy Car
the Shabby Car
the Silly Car
the Greedy Car
the Trendy Car
and the Little Square Car.

Good King Benefactor, accompanied by Queen Echo and the Lord Chancellor (who was now 210½), walked down the line to inspect each car. The Speedy Car was well-known all over the kingdom for always rushing around and nearly running people over. He was long and thin with big, white wheels and a flash of red down each side, which was supposed to make him go even faster. The King patted him on the radiator and wished him the best of Littleland luck. The Queen patted him twice. Next the royal couple came to the Flashy Car, who had a blue bonnet, red doors, green wheels, yellow upholstery and striped wheels. The King tried hard to think of something complimentary to say.

The Queen diplomatically remarked, 'What an unusual colour scheme – just like a rainbow. What an unusual colour scheme – just like a rainbow.'

They then both moved on to the Shabby Car. Once again the King was left speechless, because the car was covered with such a thick layer of dust and rust that there was no way of telling what colour the paintwork underneath really was. The only clean parts of the Shabby Car were those that had most recently been dented in crashes.

Shabby can't have had a bath for weeks, thought the King, as he pulled his ermine-trimmed cloak closely around him to be sure he didn't brush against him.

The next car in line was the Silly Car, who was actually facing the wrong direction. He was a very nice little car, but dreadfully silly. He was always doing silly things like pouring tea instead of water into his radiator, and forgetting where he was supposed to be going when he was already half way there. Nevertheless the King patted him on the boot and wished him luck. The Queen patted him twice before moving on to the Greedy Car which only made her scowl (twice).

The Greedy Car was wide and fat. He was a very expensive car to keep on the road, because he ate so much oil, and drank so much Five Star Petrol. This meant he had to spend most of his life in a garage, because he could only afford to go out for a drive on special occasions.

Next to him stood the Trendy Car who was so busy admiring his stereo speakers in his reversible rear view mirror that he nearly missed meeting the Royal party. Trendy was covered in all the latest gadgets – wire wheels, electrically operated windows, a solar-powered engine and, believe it or not, a car telephone. Good King Benefactor couldn't wait to try out the phone, so he sent Queen Echo back to the Palace with instructions to call him.

'Hello,' he said, picking up the car phone when it rang.

'Hello, hello,' replied the Queen.

'Hello, hello,' shouted the King again. It was not a very good line.

'Hello, hello, hello, hello,' repeated Queen Echo.

In fact, they might have gone on saying hello all day long, if the Lord Chancellor hadn't reminded the King tactfully that the inspection was not yet over, and the race was due to start, so the King said goodbye once and put the phone down.

'And now, Your Majesty, there is only one car left to inspect – the Little Square Car.'

'The Little Square Car?' queried the King.

'The Little Square Car? The Little Square Car?' echoed the Queen on her return, and they both looked round and stared in disbelief. And the more they stared, the more square the car seemed.

It had a square steering wheel
square engine
square seats
square lamps
square boot
square radiator
and strangest of all,
square wheels with square tyres.

Good King Benefactor continued to stare at the Little Square Car, but said nothing as he didn't want to admit that he had never actually heard of a square car, in case everyone else had. The Queen did not help matters by remaining silent, for only the second time in months, and the Lord Chancellor said nothing because the King and Queen had said nothing. Finally he plucked up the courage to speak.

'Your Majesties will, of course, know' (of course he knew they didn't know), 'of the famous Little Square Car, who comes from Rightangle, a town which is famous for making square things – like boxes, toast, television sets and . . .'

'Of course,' said the King.

'Of course, of course,' said the Queen.

The King turned aside and whispered in the Lord Chancellor's ear. 'How can the Little Square Car hope to win the Round Littleland Race while he has square wheels?'

'An interesting conundrum, Your Majesty,' said the Lord Chancellor, 'but one that I cannot answer as all that is known for certain about the Little Square Car is that he is renowned for trying hard.'

'Admirable,' said the King.

'Admirable, admirable,' said the Queen.

Before the King could think of anything else to add his watch struck twelve.

'I think the hour has come, Your Majesty,' prompted the Lord Chancellor, 'for you to carry out your duty,' and, without another word, he handed the King a large pistol and a small piece of paper.

Good King Benefactor was apprehensive, but sometimes Kings must do very brave deeds, otherwise what's the point of having a King at all? So he held the large pistol high above his head and started to read from the small piece of paper.

'This is the official Round Littleland Race to discover which is the fastest car in the kingdom. The cars will all start here at the gates of the Palace, drive once around the kingdom, and the first car to return to the Palace will be declared the winner. On your marks, get set . . .' The King then dropped the large pistol, and as it hit the ground it exploded with a noisy bang, and the seven cars roared into action.

'They're off,' came a shout from the crowd and the Speedy Car went straight into the lead, with the others following close behind, except for the Little Square Car who could only bump along slowly, which made him rather car-sick.

'It's not fair,' said the King, who was watching the race on television.

'It's not fair, it's not fair,' agreed the Queen.

'The Square Car has no hope of winning while he has square wheels; hadn't someone better tell him that?' asked the King.

They both turned to the Lord Chancellor for guidance.

The old man stroked his beard, and considered before pronouncing. 'The rules of the race do not allow for any change of design once the race has started, so no one must advise the Little Square Car to do anything about his wheels or he would be disqualified,' said the Lord Chancellor, reading out loud from the rule book. 'In any case,' he added, 'the people of Rightangle would never consider it – who ever heard of round books, round bricks or round televisions.'

The King nodded gravely in agreement.

'Quite,' he said.

'Quite, quite,' added the Queen.

So no one said anything to the Little Square Car about his little square wheels.

When the contestants reached the halfway point, Speedy had kept his lead from Trendy, who had stayed ahead of Flashy. Greedy, Silly and Shabby were in fourth, fifth and sixth places, while all the time the Little Square Car remained in last place. But he was trying so hard that the gathering crowds began to support him and cheered more loudly for the Little Square Car than for any other entrant, but even with this support he made no impression on the leaders. And then, to everyone's surprise, the Shabby Car burst a tyre and as his spare tyre was already flat he had to sit at the side of the road and wait for a break-down van. This made it possible for the Little Square Car to overtake Shabby and move up into sixth place. The crowd along the route cheered and cheered when the Little Square Car passed Shabby.

Then Silly Car, not thinking, took a wrong turning and started heading in completely the opposite direction. This was caused by the fact that he was reading his map upside down. So, the Little Square Car bumped into fifth position, and the crowds cheered once again. Meanwhile, the Greedy Car, who had never been on such a long journey before, checked his fuelometer — only to discover that he was about to run out of petrol. With an exhausted splutter his engine finally gave up and he slowly came to a halt. The Little Square Car passed him, moving into fourth place, which made the crowds cheer yet again.

Up in front of him, Flashy was distracted by a poster advertising a car fashion parade and, deciding that he had a better chance of winning that, he fell out of the race. The Little Square Car now found himself in third place, bumping along behind Trendy and Speedy.

And that's probably how it would have finished up if Trendy hadn't spotted a display of miniature car televisions in a shop window and decided he couldn't wait to have one installed immediately. The Little Square Car hurried past him with only the Speedy Car left to overtake. Speedy was now panting along, and getting more and more tired as each mile went by. It had been far too long a race for a Speedy Car.

The happy crowds were ten deep as they watched the final few miles and started to chant loudly for the Little Square Car.

'Square Car
Square Car
Square Car
Square Car!'

The Speedy Car had become so exhausted that the Little Square Car began to catch him up, edging nearer and nearer with each mile. The excitement was now reaching fever pitch as the two cars raced towards the Palace and the final mile. The Little Square Car was taking the corners like a champion and when they reached the main square, he managed to edge in front of the tired Speedy for the first time, with only half a mile to go to the finishing line and the Salt-and-pepper-pot Palace in his sights.

The crowd felt certain that the Little Square Car was going to win, as Speedy became more and more tired and started to fall further and further behind. On the Palace balcony Good King Benefactor stood waiting to greet the winner, holding in his arms the biggest cup ever made in Littleland, while Queen Echo and the Lord Chancellor sat on each side of him unable to conceal their pleasure at the way the race was turning out.

With 400 metres to go the Little Square Car still hung on to his lead, 300 metres, 200 metres, 100 metres. Surely the Little Square Car was bound to win the Round Littleland Race and the biggest cup ever made in Littleland – when suddenly and quite unexpectedly, the Little Square Car hit the edge of a roundabout and one of his wheels was knocked off and went bumping down the road all on its own. The Little Square Car, who now only had three wheels, came to a grinding halt right in front of the Palace gates.

FASTEST CAR

A dreadful hush fell over the vast crowd as Speedy swept past the Little Square Car and over the finishing line to win the race. Poor Little Square Car could only sit there, broken down, watching as one by one the other cars passed him. Finally, when all the cars had passed him, some disappointed supporters in the crowd pushed the Little Square Car over the finishing line into last place.

Good King Benefactor looked sad, Queen Echo looked doubly sad and the Lord Chancellor didn't know what to say. When the King awarded the biggest cup ever made in Littleland to the Speedy Car, the crowd hardly cheered at all because they felt the rightful winner should have been the Little Square Car from Rightangle.

In bed that night, Queen Echo was clutching her 'By Royal Appointment' hot water bottles and tossing and turning so much that Good King Benefactor couldn't get to sleep.

'What is the matter, my dear?'

'I feel so sorry for the Little Square Car going all the way back to Rightangle without a prize,' said the Queen. 'I feel so sorry for the Little Square Car going all the way back to Rightangle without a prize.'

'What am I supposed to do?' asked the King.

'Call for the Lord Chancellor,' said the Queen. 'He'll think of something. Call for the Lord Chancellor. He'll think of something.'

'In the middle of the night?' asked the King.

'In the middle of the night,' said the Queen. 'In the middle of the night.'

BY ROYAL APPOINTMENT

So the King put on his 'By Royal Appointment' dressing gown and his special matching slippers and went off in search of the Lord Chancellor. Everything that the King and Queen wore, ate or used had to be the very best of its kind and, when it had been tested, was awarded a 'By Royal Appointment' seal, so that all the people of Littleland would know how good it was.

When the King reached the Lord Chancellor's bedroom he found him, wide awake, sitting up in his four poster bed, reading the rules of car racing, trying to discover if there was any way a prize could be awarded to the Little Square Car, even though he had come last.

'The Queen is never going to let me get any sleep unless you come up with the answer. What can I do about the Little Square Car not having a prize?' asked the King.

The Lord Chancellor stroked his long white beard and considered deeply for a long time. Then he had an idea. The King, sitting on the edge of the bed, listened intently to the Lord Chancellor.

'Brilliant,' said the King, and left to tell the Queen.

'Brilliant, brilliant,' said the Queen, when she was told.

First thing the next morning, Good King Benefactor called all the cars back to the Salt-and-pepper-pot Palace in order to address them once again. The crowd that gathered outside the gates was even bigger than on the previous day. Everyone stood in silence, waiting to hear what the King had to say. The Lord Chancellor handed His Majesty a piece of paper. The King cleared his throat, as people do when they have something important to say.

'Hmmm, hmmm . . . To whom it may concern, may I just say, ladies and gentlemen and cars . . . hmmm, hmmm . . . Welcome,' said the King. 'Her Majesty Queen Echo and I have decided that it is high time we went on a Royal tour of Littleland.' The crowd cheered. 'For this tour we will need a car to travel in. It must be a very special car – a hard-working, loyal, responsible, and friendly car who will always do his best.

I do proclaim therefore that the car chosen will have the title "By Royal Appointment" and is to be the most respected car in the kingdom. And after watching the Round Littleland Race I have chosen . . .' The crowd was so quiet you could have heard a pin drop. '. . . I have chosen . . .' The Queen sneezed twice. '. . .I have chosen . . .' The Lord Chancellor held his breath, which is dangerous for someone aged 210½. '. . . I have chosen . . . the Little Square Car from Rightangle.'

The crowd went wild with delight as the King presented the Little Square Car with a special 'By Royal Appointment' square medal to stick on his bumper. (The Royal goldsmith had worked all through the night to have it ready in time.) The Queen winked twice at the Little Square Car, as she climbed into the back with Good King Benefactor. The royal couple paraded through the streets of the capital to the acclaim of the citizens. The King waved and Queen Echo waved and waved. They both had to hold on tightly because it was a very bumpy ride, but they were having such a nice time that they pretended not to notice.

So if you ever see the King and Queen out driving together, how will you be able to tell if they are in their 'By Royal Appointment' car? Yes, it will be the one with square wheels.